How Does a Rocket Work?

Have you ever blown up a balloon and then let it go? As the air rushes out, the balloon flies off. That forward motion is called **thrust**. Rockets work on the same principle. Fuel burned inside the rocket produces hot gases. As the gases expand, the pressure increases. The only place for the gases to escape is through an opening at the bottom of the rocket. When the gases rush out, the pressure is greater at the exit than in other directions, so the force pushes the rocket forward.

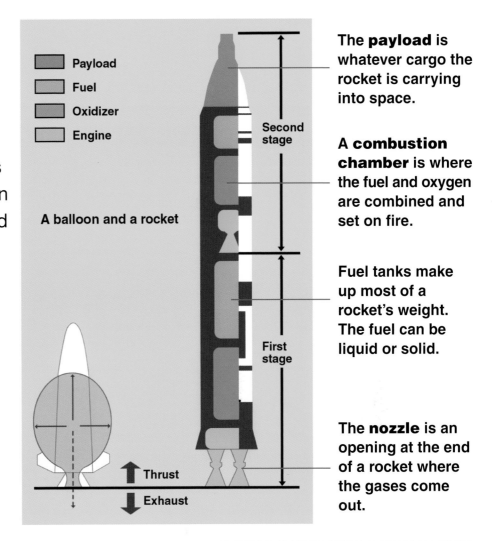

Payload
Fuel
Oxidizer
Engine

A balloon and a rocket

Second stage

First stage

Thrust

Exhaust

The **payload** is whatever cargo the rocket is carrying into space.

A **combustion chamber** is where the fuel and oxygen are combined and set on fire.

Fuel tanks make up most of a rocket's weight. The fuel can be liquid or solid.

The **nozzle** is an opening at the end of a rocket where the gases come out.

Rocket Stages

Spacecraft that travel long distances, such as into Earth's **orbit** and beyond, need a lot of fuel. That's too much for one rocket to handle, so smaller rockets, called stages, are stacked onto the main rocket. When a stage uses up its fuel, it drops away, making the rocket lighter and able to go even faster. Then the next stage takes over. Some rockets have as many as five stages.

***Saturn V* was the most powerful rocket ever built. It weighed more than 6 million pounds, and it used 11 engines. At takeoff, it burned more than 560,000 gallons of fuel in under three minutes.**

Satellites

The first spacecraft to orbit Earth was *Sputnik 1*, an **artificial satellite** that circled our planet more than one thousand times. It zoomed into space on top of a Soviet rocket on October 4, 1957. The small silver ball stayed in orbit for three months before burning up when it reentered Earth's atmosphere.

Weather Satellites

Weather satellites keep track of weather conditions all over Earth. They send back detailed images of weather patterns that help forecasters predict the next day's weather. But that's not all. Weather satellites also report on forest fires, the effects of pollution, and ocean currents.

The first weather satellite was called *TIROS-1*. It was launched in 1960.

Communications Satellite

Communications Satellites

If you watch TV programs, listen to certain radio shows, or make telephone calls, you have communications satellites to thank. Communications satellites work like a very tall radio antenna up in the sky, allowing people to instantly communicate with someone on the other side of the globe. Each satellite stays in a fixed position above Earth and orbits at the same rate as the Earth.

Navigational Satellites

Navigational satellites tell us exactly where we are on Earth. This Global Positioning System (GPS) is made up of 27 satellites spaced equally around the world. Each satellite sends out signals that tell its current location. A GPS receiver on Earth picks up signals from at least four of these satellites and uses the information to calculate its position on Earth. Sailors, pilots, drivers, and even hikers rely on GPS devices to keep them from getting lost.

Navigational Satellite

Tracking Stations

With more than 1,000 satellites in orbit, it is important to know where each one is located in order to make sure none stray off course. Tracking stations set up around the world do just that. They also receive and process information sent from satellites. A satellite's radio transmitter broadcasts its position and any data it collects to a tracking station's antennas.

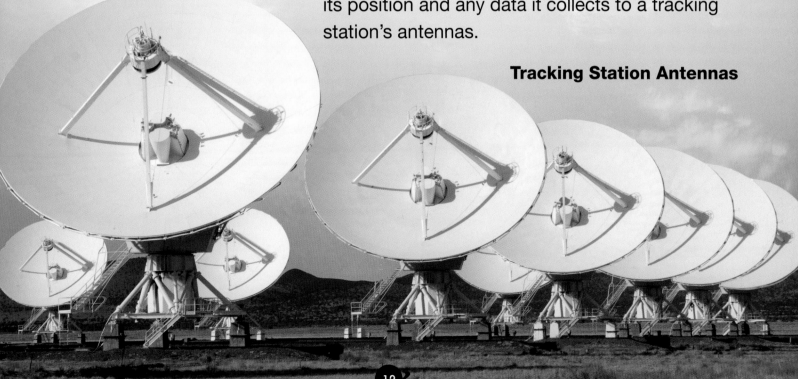

Tracking Station Antennas

Astronauts in Space

Soon after the first satellite was launched, the next challenge was to put people in space—and make sure they returned safely to Earth.

Firsts in Human Space Travel

A spacecraft called *Vostok 1* carried the first human into space. He was a Soviet named Yuri Gagarin. His historic journey into space was on April 12, 1961, and lasted just under two hours. Less than a month later, Alan B. Shephard became the first American in space. He flew in a Mercury spacecraft called *Freedom 7*. His flight was much shorter than Gagarin's, lasting just a little over 15 minutes. American John Glenn became the first American to orbit Earth in 1962. On a five-hour trip, he orbited Earth three times.

Project Mercury

NASA had one goal when it designed the one-person spacecraft for the Mercury program—to see if humans could live and work safely in space. There were six missions in all, and they went off successfully—except for one. In 1961, the hatch to *Mercury 4*'s *Liberty Bell* blew off after its splashdown into the Atlantic Ocean and the capsule sunk. Astronaut Virgil "Gus" Grissom escaped unhurt.

Mercury 4's capsule was named *Liberty Bell* because of its bell-like shape and because the name represented freedom. In 1999 the capsule was rescued from the bottom of the Atlantic Ocean.

John Glenn orbited Earth in the Mercury spacecraft *Friendship 7*. Only one person could fit inside the tiny capsule.

Project Gemini

NASA's next manned spaceflight was Project Gemini. The two-person spacecraft had ten **manned flights** between 1965 and 1966. All the missions were in preparation for an eventual trip to the moon. Gemini spacecraft went on longer flights than Mercury spacecraft, some lasting up to 13 days. Some missions practiced **docking**, or joining up, with other spacecraft. The project also had the first American **space-walkers** leave the protection of the spacecraft and venture into space.

Edward White became the first American to space-walk. He left the *Gemini 4* spacecraft and floated in space for 21 minutes.

Moonwalkers

The goal of the U.S. Apollo project was to land astronauts on the moon. Six missions achieved just that. A total of 12 astronauts have walked on the moon. The first was Neil Armstrong, who flew to the moon in the mission known as *Apollo 11*. He stepped onto the moon's surface on July 20, 1969, with the words, "That's one small step for a man, one giant leap for mankind."

Neil Armstrong's first footprint on the moon was made on the Sea of Tranquility. Because there is no wind or erosion on the moon, it is still there today, and should be there for at least another million years.

The moon's gravity is one-sixth of Earth's, so anyone walking there would feel lighter than they would on Earth. Neil Armstrong didn't find the moon's gravity a challenge, though, saying, "It's absolutely no trouble to walk around."

The Apollo 11 Spacecraft

The *Apollo 11* spacecraft had three main parts, called modules. The astronauts lived in the command module, named *Columbia*, which held all the instruments and computers. The service module had rocket engines that were used to slow down the spacecraft when it entered the moon's orbit. Otherwise, *Apollo 11* would have shot right past the moon. The third part was the lunar module, known as the *Eagle*—even though it looked more like a spider with its long legs. The *Eagle* was the only part of the spacecraft to land on the moon.

Once *Apollo 11* entered the moon's orbit, astronauts Neil Armstrong and Edwin "Buzz" Aldrin climbed into the *Eagle* and flew it down to the moon's surface. Astronaut Michael Collins remained behind in the command module, which continued to orbit the moon.

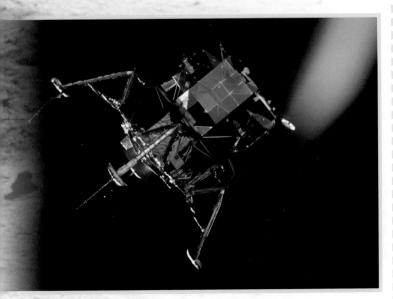

The Eagle

Splashdown

The return trip to Earth took about two and a half days. On July 24, 1969, *Columbia* splashed into the Pacific Ocean. Once in the water, its airbags opened to keep the capsule upright. After the crew left the capsule, they were helped onto a raft and then onto a helicopter.

The Apollo 11 crew sit in a raft after exiting the capsule and wait to be picked up by helicopter. The fourth man in the raft is from the United States Navy.

An electric four-wheel vehicle, called a *lunar rover,* strapped to the outside of the lunar module helped the astronauts explore more of the moon's surface than they could by walking. When the mission ended, the moon buggy stayed behind.

Training for Space

What does it take to become an astronaut and travel aboard a spacecraft? Years and years of training.

Basic Training

The first hurdle for would-be astronauts is two years of basic training. In the classroom, the trainees study space technology and science and learn about the different types of spacecraft. Trainees must also become expert scuba divers. Scuba diving prepares the future astronauts for space-walking. Moving underwater is similar to moving in space outside a spacecraft. After two years, only certain students are selected to continue.

Advanced Training

Once the trainees are finished with basic training, they are given their mission assignments. At this point, they concentrate on training in **simulators**. They also practice working aboard a full-size working model of a spacecraft.

Working in Water

To experience weightlessness, astronauts also train at the Neutral Buoyancy Laboratory (NBL) in a giant-sized pool. It is the largest indoor pool in the world. The astronauts practice moving in the pool while wearing heavy spacesuits, which can weigh up to 280 pounds. Because these special suits are worn when working outside a spacecraft, it is important astronauts know how to move in them.

Look, Ma, I'm Floating!

When a spacecraft goes into orbit, everything that is not tied down begins to float—including the astronauts. Inside a spacecraft, a floor is the same as a ceiling because there is no up or down. Astronauts can push off a wall and float all the way across the cabin. But feeling weightless is not all fun. Many astronauts report feeling nauseated. Others get headaches and feel congested when bodily fluids fill their heads due to the lack of gravity. Special training programs help the astronaut trainees get used to weightlessness.

The Vomit Comet

Since 1959, future astronauts have trained on NASA planes that simulate weightlessness. The planes fly up and down, again and again, much like a rollercoaster. When the plane descends, the astronauts inside experience weightlessness for a short amount of time. Although the plane is sometimes called the "Weightless Wonder," some who have ridden inside prefer to call it the "Vomit Comet."

These Mercury astronauts are floating inside a NASA plane.

FAST FACTS

The NBL pool holds more than 6 million gallons of water. It takes about a month to fill the pool completely.

Space Shuttles

What would it be like if every airplane was destroyed after it flew only once? For one thing, not many people would be able to fly, and almost no one would be able to afford it. That's what space travel was like before the first space shuttle was designed. Space shuttles can be launched again and again, making space travel much more efficient and much less expensive.

An Airplane or a Rocket?

A space shuttle's main part is a winged spacecraft called an **orbiter**. It looks a lot like an airplane, and it is what the astronauts ride in and where the cargo is stored. Attached to the orbiter are an outer fuel tank and a pair of booster rockets. The space shuttle is blasted into space by rocket engines on the orbiter and the booster rockets. After takeoff, the fuel tank and booster rockets drop off and land in the sea. The orbiter continues up into space.

fuel tank

booster rockets

orbiter

FAST FACTS

The *Columbia* was the first space shuttle. It took off from Cape Canaveral, Florida, in 1981.

The average space shuttle goes on about 100 missions.

Coming Back to Earth

After a space shuttle's mission is completed, it glides back to Earth. It travels at speeds up to 17,000 mph. Although the shuttle takes off like a rocket, it lands on a runway like an airplane. After a short period for maintenance, the shuttle can be launched again for another mission.

In Orbit

Once in orbit, the space shuttle carries out its mission. Sometimes a space shuttle delivers a payload to the International Space Station (ISS), launches a satellite, or brings back a satellite for repair.

The space shuttle *Atlantis* lifts the Hubble Space Telescope with its robot arm.

A Home in Space

Some people go to work in space every day. Since that would be a *very* long commute from Earth, space stations were built. Space stations let people live and work in space for long periods of time.

Home, Sweet Home

Salyut 1, the first space station, was set into orbit in 1971 by the Soviets. Two years later, *Skylab*, a United States space station, followed. Astronauts lived in the space stations for weeks and months at a time before returning to Earth. But between missions, the space stations remained empty. *Mir*, a Russian space station, changed that. For 15 years, from 1986 to 2001, it was almost always home to working astronauts.

In this photo the space station *Mir* is docked, or joined, with the U.S. space shuttle *Atlantis*. The two spacecraft held a total of ten astronauts.

The U.S., Russia, Canada, Japan, Brazil, and 11 countries in Europe are working together to build the ISS.

A World Space Station

The International Space Station (ISS) is as long as a football field. A permanent laboratory in space, the ISS performs experiments on gravity, temperature, and pressure. Launched in 1998, the ISS is still a work in progress. Because it would be much too heavy to build on Earth and then launch into space, the ISS is being put together piece by piece in space. The ISS is due to be finished in 2011.

Construction Site in Space

The ISS is made up of more than one hundred modules. Usually, the work of connecting the parts can be done inside the space station with the help of a robotic arm. But sometimes astronauts go outside the space station and attach the parts by hand. At these times, astronauts must wear insulated, pressurized spacesuits that contain supplies of oxygen.

FAST FACTS

The completed ISS will weigh almost 1 million pounds. The ISS orbits 220 miles above the Earth.

What provides the electricity for the ISS? The sun. Energy is collected on solar panels and is used to power the six laboratories onboard the station.

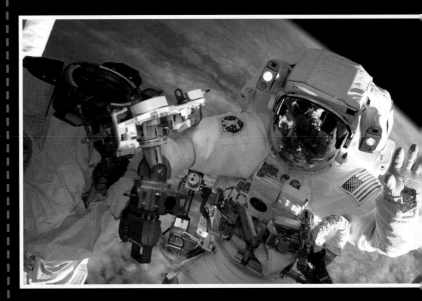

Special spacesuits protect astronauts from the harsh environment of space.

Deeper into Space

Space probes explore the solar system. These unmanned spacecraft are sent to space to do research. They take detailed photographs and gather information about planets, moons, **comets**, and **asteroids** using special cameras and instruments. Much of what scientists learn about our solar system comes from space probes. Certain probes are designed to fly past many planets and moons. Others enter a planet's or moon's orbit and study it in depth.

Voyager 1 and 2

Launched in 1977, *Voyager 1* and *2* are still flying through space on a mission to explore the outer limits of our solar system. On their way, though, the twin spacecraft took time to study the outer planets. *Voyager 1* flew past Jupiter and Saturn, sending back amazing photographs of those planets. Then the probe continued its journey deeper into space. It has now traveled more than 10.5 billion miles and is the farthest man-made object from Earth. *Voyager 2* took a grand tour of the outer solar system, visiting Jupiter, Saturn, Uranus, and Neptune. It is set to leave the solar system and enter **interstellar space** in 2015. Each spacecraft carries with it a disk that contains images and sounds from Earth, including greetings in 55 languages to any life-form it may meet.

Volcanoes in Space

One of *Voyager*'s discoveries was the eruption of volcanoes on Jupiter's moon Io. Active volcanoes had never before been seen anywhere but on Earth.

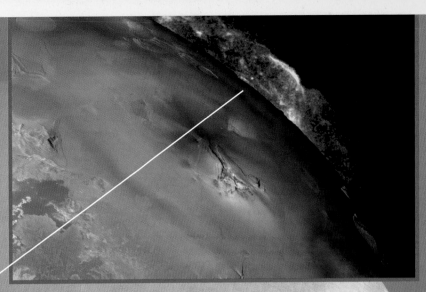

Hundreds of volcanoes are scattered throughout Io.

Messenger

Messenger, launched by NASA in 2004, is on course to study the planet Mercury. It should arrive in the planet's orbit by 2011. The probe will spend a year taking images of the entire planet. It will also collect information on Mercury's core, crust, and atmosphere. The last time a probe visited Mercury was in 1975, more than 30 years ago.

New Horizons

On its journey to Pluto, the spacecraft *New Horizons* sailed past Jupiter in 2007. It sent back images never before seen, such as lightning near Jupiter's poles and huge clumps of matter racing past the planet's rings. It is on target to reach Pluto by 2015.

Getting Even Closer

Some spacecraft probes carry smaller probes, which land on a planet or on a planet's moon. Once the probe has landed or is inside the planet's atmosphere, instruments on board conduct experiments. The information is then sent back to Earth for scientists to study.

Viking Probes

The first spacecraft to successfully land on Mars touched down in 1976. The two Viking landers sent back the first color images of Mars' rusty surface. They also scooped up soil and tested it for signs of life. The results were negative, but there is hope that future probes might show that life exists on the red planet.

Spirit and *Opportunity*

Twenty-eight years after the Viking probes, twin rovers named *Spirit* and *Opportunity* landed on Mars to explore the red planet and to look for signs of water. From Earth, scientists direct the rovers and tell them where to go. Instruments aboard each vehicle record images and take samplings of soil and rocks. In 2009 the rovers made an exciting discovery: Evidence of water was found on Mars.

The rovers were meant to run for just a few months, but they have lasted for years. *Spirit* became trapped in sand in 2010, but *Opportunity* is still going strong. It has been working on Mars for more than six years.

Giotto

FAST FACTS

The Japanese spacecraft *Hayabusa*, launched in 2003, went on a seven-year journey of 4 billion miles to become the first spacecraft to land on an asteroid and return to Earth. The asteroid, Itokawa, is just 1,640 feet long.

Giotto

In 1986 *Giotto* became the first spacecraft to get close to a comet's nucleus, or center. *Giotto* passed within 375 miles of the core of Halley's Comet. A camera on the spacecraft sent back more than 2,000 pictures. From the mission, scientists learned that comets are made up mostly of dust with a small amount of ice.

Cassini

The spacecraft *Cassini* began its orbit around Saturn in 2004. It is studying the planet and its rings and many of its moons. In 2005 it dropped a probe onto the surface of Titan, a moon of Saturn.

This computer illustration shows the *Cassini* spacecraft firing its engine as it gets ready to orbit Saturn.

Looking Ahead

What is the future for space travel? There are many exciting projects in the works. Will astronauts land on Mars in the next 20 years? Will new ideas for rockets be successful? Will we be taking our vacations in space hotels?

Elevator to the Stars

Space engineers are developing a new way to get people into space without rockets. A space elevator would be used instead! The space elevator would allow a spacecraft to climb a cable into the sky. Made of a paper-thin yet incredibly strong and flexible material, a ribbon-shaped cable would reach more than 60,000 miles into space up to a platform. The bottom of the cable would be anchored in the sea. People and cargo would ride up the elevator on mechanical lifters. Once at the top, they would transfer to a traditional spacecraft and head off to their final destination.

Spacecraft That Fix Themselves

If you get a scratch or cut, your body's immune system kicks in and gets to work healing the wound. Imagine if a spacecraft could do the same! Now when spacecraft are punctured by tiny bits of space debris or develop hairline cracks, the damage worsens unless repaired immediately. Scientists are working on a new type of synthetic compound that can heal itself when damaged. Spacecraft made with this new material will be able to venture far into space without repair worries.

Solar Sails

A spacecraft's weight is about 95 percent rocket fuel, making space flight extremely expensive. But what if there were a way to reduce the amount of fuel by harnessing the sun's energy to propel spacecraft once they've reached space? Space engineers are experimenting with solar–sail powered spacecraft in the hope of making space flight more affordable. The sails being tested are made of lightweight, reflective materials. Light particles bounce off the sails constantly, pushing them forward at a faster and faster speed.

Glossary

artificial satellite a man-made object launched into space that travels around a planet or a moon

asteroid a small or large rock found especially between the orbits of Mars and Jupiter

atmosphere the layers of gases that surround a star or a planet

combustion chamber the part of a rocket where fuel and oxygen are combined and ignited

comet a frozen ball of dust and gas that develops one or more long tails when near the sun

constellation a grouping of stars

docking the joining of one spacecraft to another in space

gravity the invisible force between objects that causes objects to attract each other

interstellar space the regions of space beyond the planets of the solar system

manned flight spacecraft that carries people aboard

nozzle an opening at the end of a rocket where gases exit

orbit a path followed by an object in space; to go around another object in a single path

orbiter the part of the space shuttle that carries the crew and the payload

payload cargo carried aboard spacecraft

rocket a machine used to launch spacecraft into space

simulator a machine that lets the user train under conditions similar to real life

solar system the Sun and all the planets, moons, and other space objects bound to the sun by gravity

space probe an unmanned spacecraft that carries instruments to record facts about space

space-walker an astronaut who moves about in space outside a spacecraft

thrust a force from a rocket that propels a spacecraft forward

Index